BIRBAL, TH

THE THIEF'S STICK

BIRBAL WAS A MINISTER AT THE COURT OF THE GREAT MUGHAL EMPEROR, AKBAR. HE WAS OFTEN CALLED UPON TO DISPENSE JUSTICE.

ONCE, A RICH MERCHANT OF DELHI CAME TO HIM WITH A COMPLAINT.

HUZUR, A BAG CONTAINING ALL MY MONEY HAS BEEN STOLEN. PLEASE HELP ME FIND THE THIEF.

WHOM DO YOU SUSPECT?

I THINK ONE OF MY SERVANTS COULD BE THE THIEF. BUT WITHOUT BEING CERTAIN, HOW CAN I TAKE ANY ACTION?

BIRBAL THOUGHT FOR A WHILE. THEN—

IF THE THIEF IS ONE OF YOUR SERVANTS, WE CAN EASILY FIND HIM OUT.

THE NEXT DAY THE MERCHANT TOOK HIS SEVEN SERVANTS WITH HIM TO BIRBAL'S HOUSE.

A MAGICIAN HAS GIVEN ME THESE STICKS; THEY HELP TO DETECT THIEVES.

EACH OF THE SERVANTS WAS GIVEN A STICK.

IF ANY ONE OF THESE STICKS IS TOUCHED BY A THIEF IT WILL GROW BY EXACTLY AN INCH, OVERNIGHT.

YOU WILL ALL BE GIVEN SEPARATE ROOMS TO STAY IN. WHEN WE MEET TOMORROW, WE WILL KNOW WHO THE THIEF IS.

THE SERVANTS WERE SHOWN THEIR ROOMS.

NEXT MORNING, THE SERVANTS WERE BROUGHT BEFORE BIRBAL.

NOW MEASURE THE STICKS ONE BY ONE.

HUZUR, THIS STICK IS SHORTER BY ONE INCH.

THAT MAN IS THE THIEF! ARREST HIM!

BUT HUZUR, YOU SAID YESTERDAY THAT THE STICK WOULD GROW BY AN INCH.

BECAUSE I SAID THAT, THE REAL THIEF CUT HIS STICK SHORT BY ONE INCH... EXACTLY WHAT I HAD EXPECTED HIM TO DO.

THE THIEF WAS PUT IN JAIL, AND THE MERCHANT WAS HAPPY THAT JUSTICE HAD BEEN RENDERED.

THE OILMAN AND THE BUTCHER

ONCE, AN OILMAN AND A BUTCHER CAME TO BIRBAL WITH A COMPLAINT.

BIRBAL FIRST HEARD THE BUTCHER.

HUZUR, I WAS BUSY SELLING MEAT WHEN THIS OILMAN ENTERED MY SHOP.

"...HE WANTED TO SELL OIL TO ME...

WAIT HERE, WHILE I FETCH A VESSEL FOR THE OIL.

"WHEN I WENT IN, HE QUIETLY PICKED UP MY MONEY BAG...

"...AND RAN AWAY WITH IT."

I RAN AFTER HIM AND RETRIEVED MY BAG, BUT HE STILL CLAIMS THAT IT IS HIS.

HUZUR, I DID ENTER HIS SHOP. BUT THE REST OF HIS STORY IS NOT TRUE. IT WAS LIKE THIS.

"HE PAID FOR THE OIL HE HAD BOUGHT...

"...WHEN I OPENED MY MONEY BAG TO PUT IN THE MONEY I HAD RECEIVED FROM HIM...

SO MUCH MONEY.

"HE BECAME GREEDY AND SEIZED MY MONEY BAG...

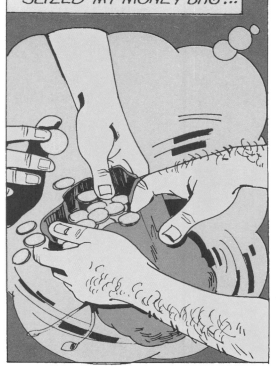

"...I RAN AFTER HIM AND CAUGHT UP WITH HIM. BUT HE REFUSED TO GIVE MY MONEY BACK TO ME."

THE OFFICERS WERE BAFFLED.

HOW CAN BIRBAL GIVE THE VERDICT IN A CASE LIKE THIS?

GO, AND GET A TUB OF HOT WATER.

PUT THE MONEY BAG IN THE TUB.

NOW LET ME INSPECT THE WATER.

HMM...THERE ARE DROPS OF OIL IN THE WATER. THE DROPS COME FROM THE MONEY BAG.

SUCH AN OILY MONEY BAG COULD ONLY BELONG TO AN OILMAN. SEIZE THE BUTCHER AND SEND HIM TO PRISON.

THE RELIABLE WITNESS

AN OLD MAN WENT ON A PILGRIMAGE AFTER GIVING A BAG CONTAINING A THOUSAND GOLD COINS TO HIS FRIEND FOR SAFE-KEEPING.

WHEN HE RETURNED—

FRIEND, I AM BACK HOME. PLEASE RETURN MY BAG.

WHAT BAG ARE YOU TALKING ABOUT? YOU NEVER GAVE ME ANY.

THE BAG CONTAINED ALL MY SAVINGS. PLEASE DON'T JOKE WITH ME. GIVE ME MY BAG.

WHAT BAG ARE YOU TALKING ABOUT? YOU NEVER GAVE ME ANY, YOU OLD FOOL.

THE OLD MAN WAS PERPLEXED.

HOW CAN A TREE COME HERE AS A WITNESS? BUT IF I DON'T GO, BIRBAL WILL BE ANGRY.

SO HE LEFT FOR THE GROVE.

MEANWHILE, IN BIRBAL'S PALACE—

WE HAVE BEEN WAITING FOR THE OLD MAN FOR MORE THAN AN HOUR.

BE PATIENT. HE WILL SOON BE BACK.

HOW CAN THE OLD MAN BE BACK SOON? HE COULD NOT EVEN HAVE REACHED THE PLACE.

IS THE MANGO GROVE FAR FROM HERE?

IT IS MORE THAN THREE MILES AWAY.

WELL, WE SHALL WAIT TILL HE RETURNS.

HOURS LATER, THE OLD MAN RETURNED.

WHAT HAPPENED?

HUZUR, I REPEAT-ED YOUR ORDER THRICE TO THE TREE. BUT IT DID NOT MOVE.

DON'T WORRY. THAT MANGO TREE HAS ALREADY BORNE WITNESS.

BIRBAL NOW TURNED TO THE OLD MAN'S FRIEND—

YOU ARE A LIAR! THE OLD MAN DID GIVE THE MONEY BAG TO YOU. HOW ELSE COULD YOU KNOW WHICH GROVE HE WAS GOING TO AND HOW FAR AWAY IT WAS?

THE MASTER AND HIS SLAVE

ONE DAY, THE KOTWAL OF DELHI BROUGHT TWO MEN TO AKBAR'S COURT

JAHANPANAH, THE KAZI COULD NOT RESOLVE THE DISPUTE BETWEEN THESE TWO MEN. SO I HAVE BROUGHT THEM HERE.

THE EMPEROR RECOGNISED ONE OF THE MEN.

SHER ALI, WHAT BRINGS YOU HERE?

JAHANPANAH! AS YOU ARE AWARE, I AM A TRADER AND I HAVE BEEN IN DELHI FOR MORE THAN FIVE YEARS.

13

... YOU MUST HAVE BEEN MASQUERADING AS SHER ALI, NASIBA.

BE QUIET. BIRBAL WILL DECIDE YOUR CASE.

NASIBA? HOW DARE YOU CALL ME NASIBA!

I WILL CLOSE MY EYES AND MEDITATE. I WILL SOON KNOW WHO THE LIAR IS. MEANWHILE, BOTH OF YOU MUST LIE FLAT ON YOUR STOMACH ON THE FLOOR.

BIRBAL SUDDENLY OPENED HIS EYES.

I KNOW THE TRUTH NOW. CALL IN THE EXECUTIONER.

WHEN THE EXECUTIONER CAME WITH HIS AXE—

CHOP OFF THE SLAVE'S HEAD.

NOW THE GUILTY ONE IS BOUND TO REACT.

AS THE EXECUTIONER RAISED HIS AXE...

...THE DELHI MERCHANT SPRANG TO HIS FEET.

HUZUR, SPARE MY LIFE.

ALL THE PROPERTY OF THE MAN, POSING AS SHER ALI WAS RESTORED TO THE REAL OWNER, AND NASIBA WAS IMPRISONED.

BIRBAL'S
KHICHDI *

ONCE, DURING WINTER, AKBAR, BIRBAL AND A FEW COURTIERS STOPPED FOR A WHILE NEAR A LAKE, A COUPLE OF MILES AWAY FROM THE PALACE.

AS AKBAR STEPPED INTO THE ICE-COLD LAKE TO WASH HIS HANDS AND FEET, AN IDEA STRUCK HIM.

ANYONE, WHO CAN STAND IN THIS ICE-COLD WATER UPTO HIS NECK FOR ONE WHOLE NIGHT, WILL RECEIVE 50,000 GOLD COINS FROM ME.

JAHANPANAH! NO ONE WHO SPENDS THE WHOLE NIGHT IN THIS ICE-COLD WATER CAN SURVIVE. LET THE CONDITIONS BE SOMEWHAT EASIER.

NO. I WILL NOT CHANGE THE CONDITIONS.

A POOR BRAHMAN, WHO HAD HEARD THE EMPEROR, DEBATED WITH HIMSELF.

IF I TRY, I MIGHT DIE. ON THE OTHER HAND, IF I SURVIVE TILL MORNING, MY FAMILY WILL GET 50,000 GOLD COINS.

HE STEPPED FORWARD.

JAHANPANAH, I AM PREPARED TO ACCEPT YOUR CHALLENGE.

GOOD! I WILL LEAVE TWO GUARDS AS WITNESSES.

THE POOR BRAHMAN SPENT THE WHOLE NIGHT IN THE COLD LAKE.

AT SUNRISE, HE CAME OUT OF THE WATER.

GUARDS! PLEASE TAKE ME TO THE EMPEROR.

THE GUARDS BROUGHT HIM TO THE COURT.

JAHANPANAH, I HAVE SPENT THE WHOLE NIGHT IN THE LAKE.

YES, JAHANPANAH! WHAT THE BRAHMAN SAYS IS TRUE.

WELL THEN, LET HIM BE GIVEN 50,000 GOLD COINS, AS PROMISED BY ME.

BUT A JEALOUS COURTIER INTERVENED.

TELL ME, O BRAHMAN, HOW DID YOU SPEND THE NIGHT?

AS I HAVE ALREADY SAID — I SPENT THE NIGHT IN THE WATER.

WERE YOU LOOKING AT ANYTHING?

WELL, I SPENT PART OF THE TIME LOOKING AT THE PALACE LIGHTS.

IN THAT CASE, YOU DID DERIVE WARMTH FROM THE PALACE LIGHTS. YOU DIDN'T FULFIL THE CONDITIONS. YOU DO NOT DESERVE THE REWARD.

THIS WAS UNFAIR, BUT THE EMPEROR DID NOT UTTER A WORD AS THE BRAHMAN LOOKED TO HIM FOR JUSTICE.

BIRBAL, HOWEVER, MADE A VOW.

I WILL SEE TO IT THAT THE POOR MAN GETS HIS DUE.

A FEW DAYS LATER, BIRBAL INVITED AKBAR AND A FEW COURTIERS TO DINNER.

AFTER A COUPLE OF HOURS, WHEN THE EMPEROR SAW THAT THERE WAS NO SIGN OF FOOD—

BIRBAL, WE ARE HUNGRY. WHY DO YOU KEEP US WAITING?

THE KHICHDI IS TAKING A LONG TIME TO COOK.

THREE HOURS LATER—

HOW LONG DO YOU THINK IT WILL BE BEFORE YOUR KHICHDI IS READY?

LET'S GO AND SEE.

BIRBAL LED THE EMPEROR AND THE COURTIERS TO HIS BACKYARD.

JAHANPANAH! THAT IS THE POT IN WHICH THE KHICHDI IS BEING COOKED.

THE WICKED KAZI

IN THE DAYS OF AKBAR, THE PEOPLE HAD RESPECT FOR KAZIS, FOR THEY WERE THE OFFICIALS APPOINTED BY THE EMPEROR TO SETTLE DISPUTES. BUT THE KAZI OF DELHI WAS A DISHONEST MAN.

ONE DAY, A POOR WOMAN CAME TO HIM.

SIR, PLEASE KEEP THIS BAG IN YOUR CUSTODY TILL I RETURN FROM MY PILGRIMAGE. IT CONTAINS A THOUSAND GOLD COINS.

HAVE YOU SEALED THE BAG?

YES, I HAVE.

THE KAZI WENT IN AND BROUGHT THE BAG.

HERE IS YOUR BAG.

INSPECT THE SEAL BEFORE YOU TAKE THE BAG AWAY.

IT'S INTACT. THANK YOU, SIR.

AND THE OLD WOMAN WENT HOME.

THERE, WHEN SHE OPENED THE BAG—

GOOD LORD! THESE ARE ONLY FLAT ROUND STONES! WHAT HAPPENED TO MY GOLD COINS?

SHE CAME WAILING TO THE KAZI.

BIBI, I DON'T KNOW WHAT YOUR BAG CONTAINED. ALL I KNOW IS THAT YOU GAVE ME A SEALED BAG, AND YOU TOOK IT BACK.

THE OLD WOMAN APPEALED TO THE EMPEROR FOR JUSTICE.

JAHANPANAH! THE BAG CONTAINED ALL MY SAVINGS. I HAVE BEEN CHEATED BY THE KAZI.

THE KAZI STUCK TO HIS STATEMENT.

JAHANPANAH! THE WOMAN GAVE ME A SEALED BAG. WHEN SHE TOOK IT BACK, THE SEAL WAS INTACT. I HAD NO IDEA WHAT THE BAG CONTAINED.

LATER, WHEN THE EMPEROR WAS ALONE WITH BIRBAL—

JAHANPANAH, IT SEEMS TO ME THAT THE KAZI TORE OPEN THE BAG AND THEN HAD IT DARNED BY A CLEVER DARNER.

NEXT MORNING AS SUGGESTED BY BIRBAL, AKBAR TORE A CORNER OF HIS BEDSHEET.

AT NIGHT, WHEN HE ENTERED THE BED-ROOM —

WHY, THE SHEET HAS BEEN DARNED SO PERFECTLY THAT I JUST CAN'T BELIEVE IT WAS EVER TORN. WHO DARNED IT?

THE SERVANT EXPLAINED.

JAHANPANAH, FOR FEAR OF BEING PUNISHED, I WENT TO THE CLEVEREST DARNER IN THE TOWN.

BRING HIM TO THE COURT TOMORROW.

THE MANGO TREE

ONCE TWO FARMERS, RAMU AND SHAMU CAME TO BIRBAL SEEKING JUSTICE.

HUZUR, THERE IS A MANGO TREE ON THE EDGE OF MY FARM. IT HAS ALWAYS BELONGED TO ME. NOW SHAMU CLAIMS IT IS HIS.

HUZUR, THE TREE RIGHTFULLY BELONGS TO ME. I HAVE WATERED IT FROM THE TIME IT WAS A SAPLING.

YOU MAY GO HOME NOW. BUT PRESENT YOURSELVES HERE TOMORROW.

AS SOON AS THE TWO FARMERS LEFT, BIRBAL SENT FOR A TRUSTED SERVANT.

GO TO THEIR HOUSES AT DUSK AND TELL THEM THAT SOME MANGOES ARE BEING STOLEN BY THIEVES. REPORT THEIR REACTIONS TO ME.

WHEN RAMU HEARD THE NEWS—

I HAVE SOME URGENT WORK NOW. I WILL LOOK INTO THE MATTER LATER.

AS SOON AS SHAMU HEARD THE NEWS HE RAN OUT TOWARDS THE TREE WITH A STICK IN HIS HAND.

THE NEXT DAY AT BIRBAL'S COURT—

THE TREE OBVIOUSLY CANNOT BELONG TO BOTH OF YOU. PLEASE TELL ME THE TRUTH—TO WHOM DOES IT BELONG?

TO ME!

TO ME!

SINCE I FIND IT DIFFICULT TO SETTLE THIS DISPUTE, I ORDER THAT THE MANGOES BE PLUCKED AND DIVIDED EQUALLY BETWEEN THE TWO OF YOU.

AS FOR THE TREE, IT WILL BE CUT DOWN AND THE WOOD, TOO, WILL BE EQUALLY DIVIDED.

RAMU FELT HAPPY AT THIS JUDGEMENT.

YOU ARE FAIR AND JUST.

HUZUR, I HAVE TENDED THAT TREE FOR SEVEN YEARS. I CAN'T SEE IT HEWN DOWN. LET THE TREE GO TO RAMU.

SHAMU, I DECLARE YOU TO BE THE RIGHTFUL OWNER. LET RAMU BE WHIPPED FOR TELLING A LIE.